HERE TODAY
gone tomorrow

a book of poetry and reflection

Peace Mbuashu-Ndip

HERE TODAY
gone tomorrow

a book of poetry and reflection

Written By: Peace Mbuashu-Ndip
Designed By: Nalani Butler & Aaron C. Butler

ISBN: 9798991412148 (Paperback)
ISBN: 9798991412155 (eBook)
Library of Congress Control Number: 2024923165

Printed in the United States of America

BookButler Publishing Company
Upper Marlboro, MD 20774

TheBookButler.com

BookButler Publishing Company titles may be purchased in bulk for
educational, business, fundraising, or sales promotional use. For
information, please email: info@thebookbutler.com

Table of Contents

IV

The Beginning

The beginning of this book starts on page one
And it will not end 'til I say it is done

The beginning is where everything starts
As I slowly make my way into your heart
In this book, you will experience many emotions
With wonderful poems that flow like the ocean

I'm just a girl writing a book
I'm exploring new territories and taking a look
I'm human and I make mistakes
I try to stay calm - still like a lake

Hopefully, you find this book appealing
Leaving you with a sense of healing

This is the end of this poem but not the end of the book
This book tells a story - a message you hopefully took
Go on and read now, hope you have fun
OK for real now, this poem is done

I Have a Story

Page by page
Chapter by chapter
I have a story
Word by word
Crying and laughter
I have a story

From front cover to back
From one to many paragraphs
My story will go on and on
Even if I don't live that long

I am important
Beautiful like my mother
I am smart
Passionate like my father

I am black and beautiful
Strong and proud
I can be a lot and a handful
Stubborn and loud

Look around - everyone has a story
It can be dark or gloomy or filled with glory
People are like puzzles, waiting to be solved
Put the pieces together, now they've evolved

My story hasn't finished
And hopefully won't soon
I'll fill out every chapter
Me - a girl from Cameroon

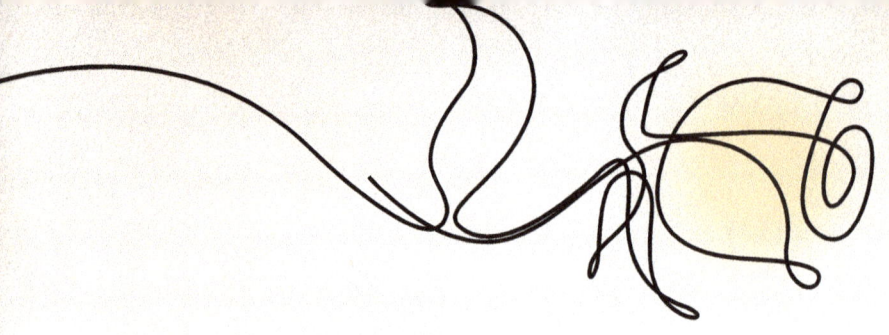

What's your story?

_____

_____

_____

_____

_____

_____

_____

_____

_____

_____

_____

_____

_____

_____

_____

_____

_____

_____

_____

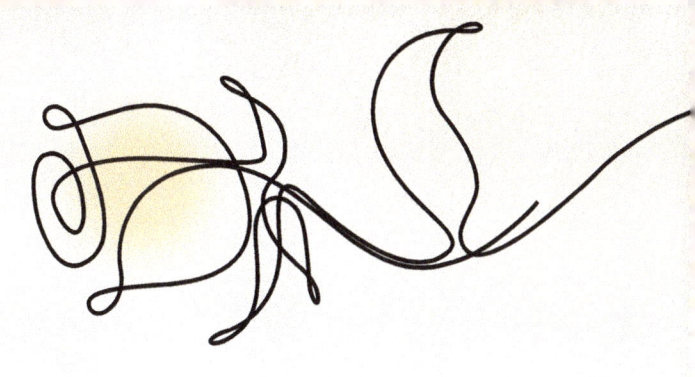

Music

The ink from the pen flows as I write
A new song comes alive, I write with delight

Music is beautiful
The words and lyrics
That catchy melody in your brain which sticks

I love writing songs
I can make my ideas come alive
It's like an egg hatching
The idea hatches - a song is born
As the song grows, I add ideas, melody, and tune
The vocals are sweet
The instrumental is nice
Music can be anything you want it to be
From culture to culture, brain to brain

I can express myself through music and I love that
It can be interpreted in different ways
But can also send a direct message to someone

Musicals are music but more
There's more acting and creativity
A musical includes lots of different types of music
And there are so many genres

Rap, Classical, Hip-Hop
Jazz, Reggae, and Pop

Music is anything, my everything
That's why I love music

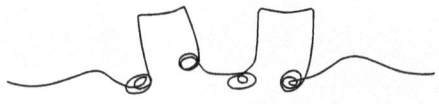

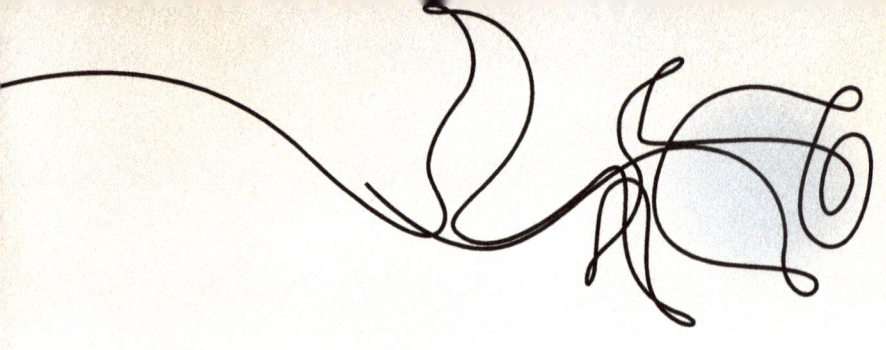

What songs resonate most with you, and what feelings or memories do they bring up?

_____

_____

_____

_____

_____

_____

_____

_____

_____

_____

_____

_____

_____

_____

_____

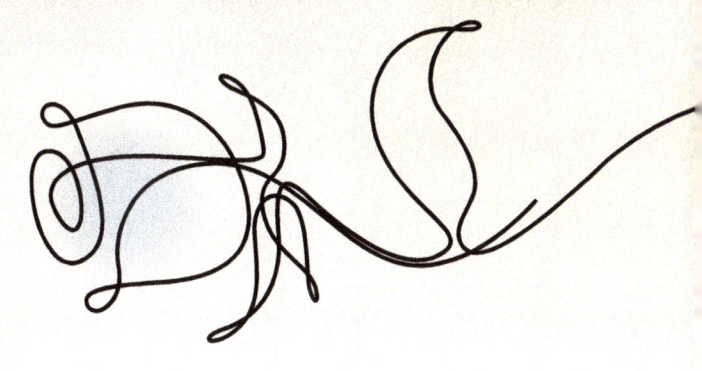

Writing Thee Poem

I wanna write THEE Poem
That "I like that line" kinda poem
That "That poem was fine" kinda poem
That "I should read that one more time" kinda poem
That "I really liked that rhyme"
Kind of poem

I wanna write about heartbreak
And heartache
My real best friends and the real fake
I wanna make people cry, both for good and bad
I wanna make people feel things, both the happy and the sad

I wanna write an apology poem to say sorry
Yeah, I said what I said, but I didn't have to say it like that
This poem has to be great
I wanna read this and say, "Yeah, I ate"

I wanna write the poem that encourages people
I wanna write the poem that has a message for the people
I wanna write the poem that explains love, that explains hate, that explains everything that's on your mind
I wanna write the poem that is special
I wanna write the poem that says what you're thinking
I wanna pull the words right out of your brain and your heart

I wanna write the poem so sour it attracts my enemies
I wanna write the poem so sweet it attracts honeybees
I wanna write the poem where the words stick with you so you won't forget me
I wanna write a poem so strong the words are bullets to the soul
So strong you never forget it
So strong you never forget me
Or what I did, have done, or are bound to do
I refuse to die a mere occupant of the earth
Refusal to being forgotten

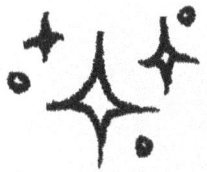

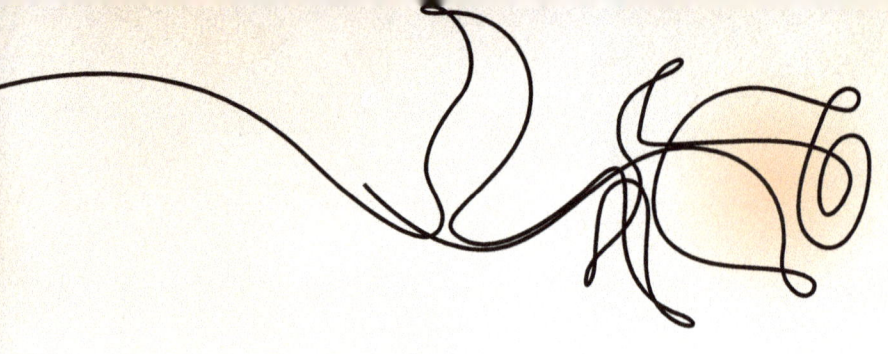

What is something YOU hope to accomplish?

_____

_____

_____

_____

_____

_____

_____

_____

_____

_____

_____

_____

_____

_____

_____

_____

What it Means to Be a Black Girl

What it means to be a black girl
It means you're pretty
I'm talking when the sun hits your melanin-filled skin
it shines like gold outside and within
kind of pretty

What it means to be a black girl
It means you are smart
I'm talking my brain is almost bigger than my heart
kinda smart

What it means to be a black girl
It means you work hard
Just like my momma and dad did to give me a great life

What it means to be a black girl
It means you struggle like any human being
What it means to be a black girl
It means you make mistakes like any human being
What it means to be a black girl
It means you are a human being

What it means to be a human being
It means you have skin, whether it's colored or not
It means you aren't the same but should be treated rightfully
It means you're special, even if you don't know it you are

What it means to be a black girl
Is that you're a beautiful human being.
Just like those before us

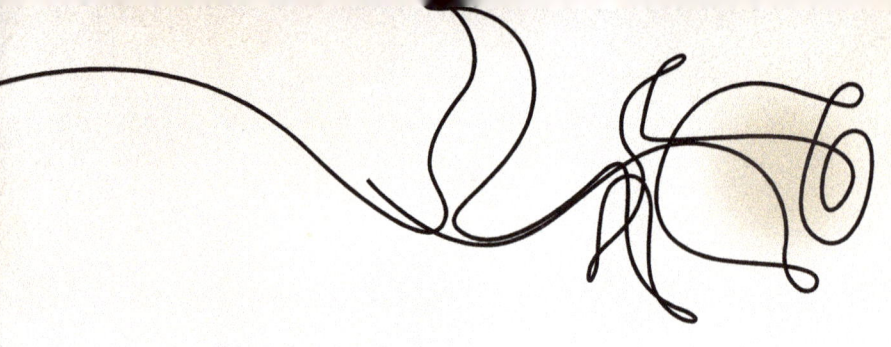

What does your race and culture mean to you?

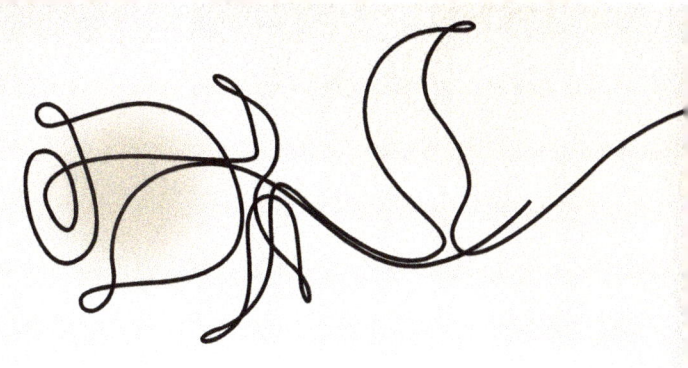

It's Okay

Drop by drop my tears form a pool
and the darkness inside me brings me to a cruel
State of mind
Where I can't find
Solid ground to stand on

It lurks behind me
The rejection of happiness around me
All these feelings surround me
And when no one is here
You lend me a listening ear
You appear
And you tell me, "It's Okay"

You say that I have nothing to fear, "It's Okay"
The sky isn't gloomy anymore - it's clear, "It's Okay"
I will always love you as my peer, "It's Okay"
Just know that I have cherished you dear, "It's Okay"
Every year, "Because It's Okay"
"You're Okay"
"We will all be Okay"

And what do I say?
I say
Okay

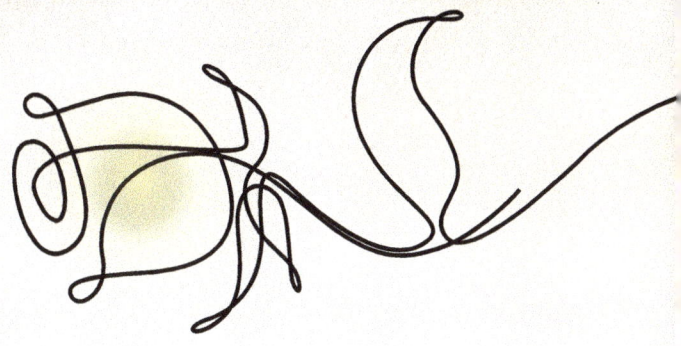

Reflect on your support system. Who is always there when you need them?

Death

Death. What is death?
Is it when you say your goodbyes, for the very last time?
Or when you realize that no longer can you climb this lifeline?

Is death our destiny?
If so, don't you want to be remembered?
I want to be remembered, create a legacy.

Legacy. What is a legacy?
Is it how you'll remember me?
As a little girl named Peace?
Life is gift. Any day could be your last
So I'm living it to the fullest
Not focused on the past

Everybody is going to be dead one day
Just give them time
My day could come soon
Until then, I'll wait on mine

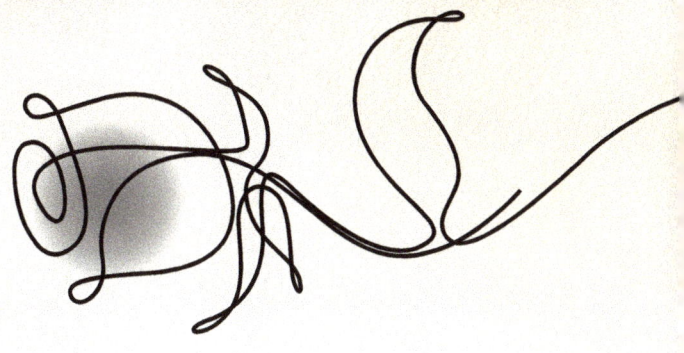

What do you think makes life special?

_____
_____
_____
_____
_____
_____
_____
_____
_____
_____
_____
_____
_____
_____
_____
_____

Don't You See

Don't you see she's hurting?
She cries every night
Don't you see she's beautiful?
A majestic sight
Don't you see she's human?
She makes mistakes
Don't you see she's bendable?
But soon she'll break

Can't you tell she's strong?
Stubborn with pride
Can't you tell she's lively?
But on the inside she died
Can't you tell she's trying?
Though on the inside she's dying

You tell her to bend
She bends 'til she breaks
You tell her to smile
But the smile is fake
You tell her she's a great person
But you don't mean it
Even if she knows she is
She'll never admit

Don't you see she's just a girl?
Still a child
It's okay to be young
Just don't get too wild

Just leave her alone let her be
'Cause you don't understand
No you don't, you really don't see
It's like her happiness was banned

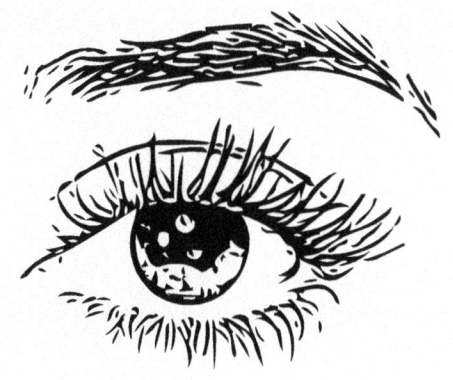

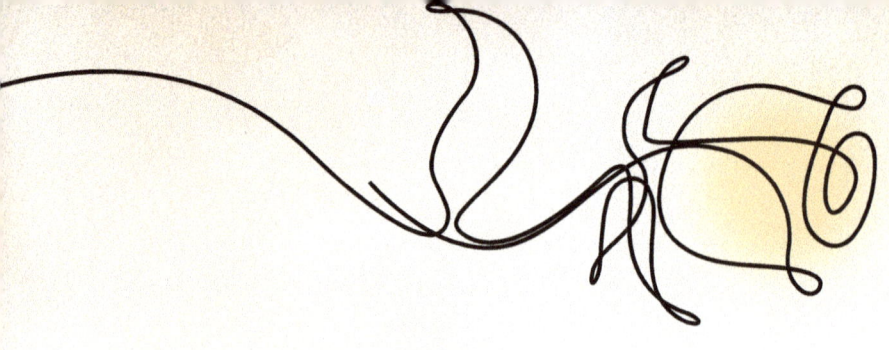

What are some thoughts or feelings that weigh on you?

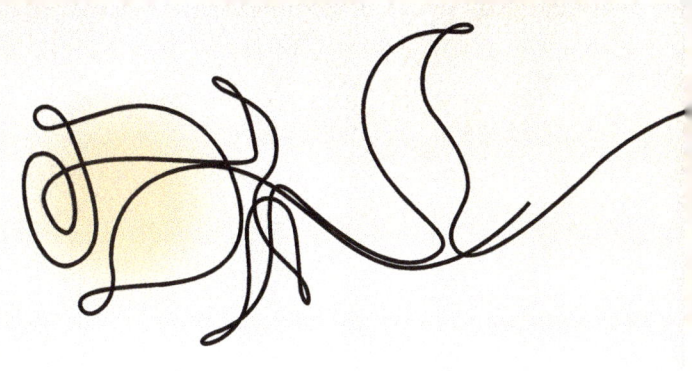

Fall

CRACKLE! BOOM! SNAP! POP!
Fall is a time to be free
CRUNCH! POW! OOPS! STOP!
Don't mess up my raked pile of leaves

The leaves fall. It's that time again
Piles of leaves fall from trees
It's fall
The pumpkin spice, cinnamon, and apple scents fill the air
It's fall
The leaves are yellow and orange and red as the green disappears
It's fall

It's getting chilly out, might wanna wear a jacket
Layer up for the wind blows cooler than before
The burning hot weather of summer is gone
The bright green left
We are left with the crunchy leaves
We go from tank tops to sweater weather
It's fall

If you fall it's in a soft pile of leaves
Then rake them up again
Thanksgiving is also coming soon
Super excited
Plus my birthday is in November
A time of celebration

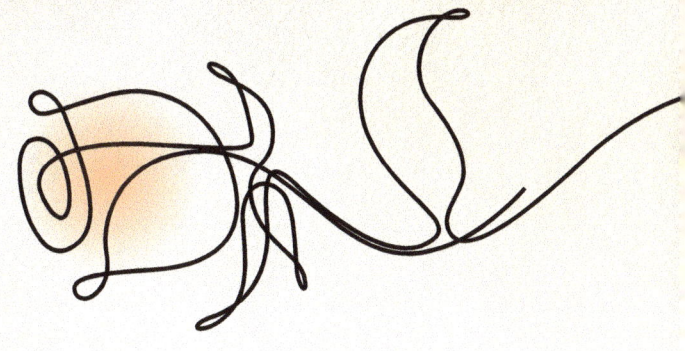

What's your favorite thing about fall?

Winter

Brr it's cold, winter is here
Time to bring out the Christmas cheer
Hanukkah and Kwanzaa are coming too
The next year begins, we start anew

Look outside, it's snowing
It covers the trees which have stopped growing
Let's build a snowman, in the wintery snow
AND WATCH OUT OVER THERE IT'S A SNOWBALL, WOAH!

Ole St. Nick with his cherry button nose
'Twas the night before Christmas when Santa would show
Gifts and presents under the tree
And the 25th will be filled with glee

January now, it's a new year
At 12 am, shout a cheer
New Year's resolutions try to fulfill
Whatever it is, fulfill you will
Mom and Dad loved family time, but kids are going back to school
Kids are off of winter break - which stinks- it isn't cool

February now, it's getting warmer and the snow is melting
Are those leaves I see? I'm telling you it's starting to look like it is
Spring

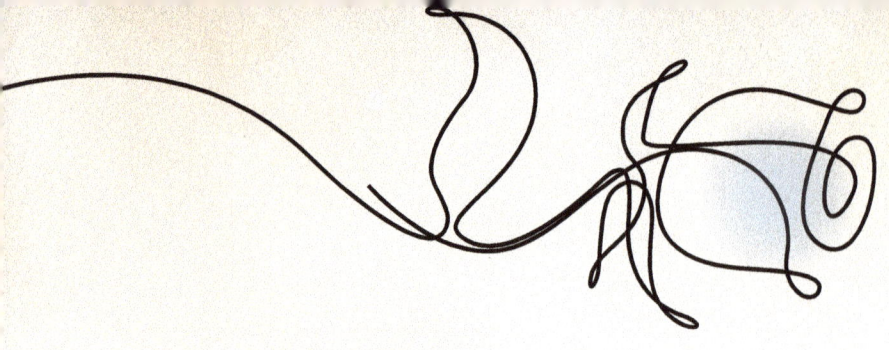

Which winter traditions mean the most to you?

_____

_____

_____

_____

_____

_____

_____

_____

_____

_____

_____

_____

_____

_____

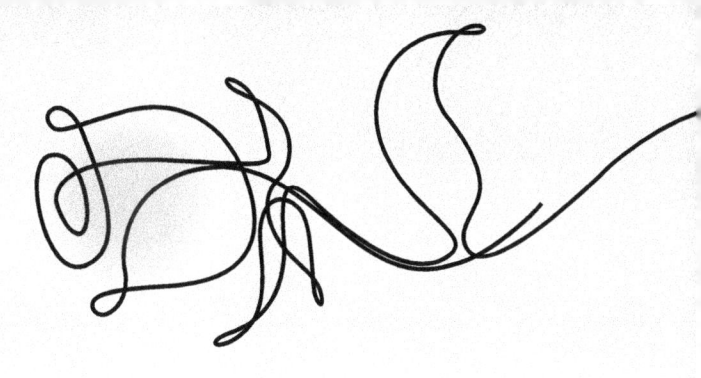

Spring

It's time for spring
Plants are blooming
Sky is blue and the trees are green
The flowers, the blossoms
And everything is awesome

The little baby animals are so adorable
But the sting from bees, in my opinion, are horrible

Butterflies
In the sky
Flying ever so joyfully
They fly so high
Wings filled with pride
Flying ever so royally

The bees buzz
The birds chirp
Flowers bloom
And rain fills the dirt
It's spring
There's rain and there's sunshine
Say goodbye to the Christmas Pine
It's spring

Easter Eggs
Easter Eggs
Let's go hunting
Because it is Spring
And everything
Is a beautiful thing
Bring on the new things
Because it is spring

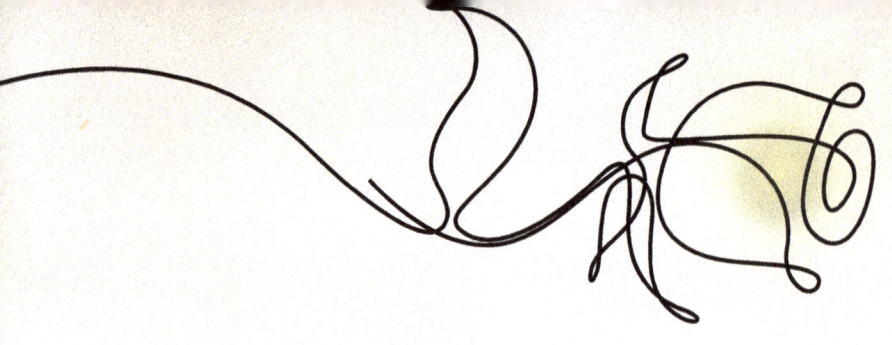

What do you think spring teaches us about change and growth?

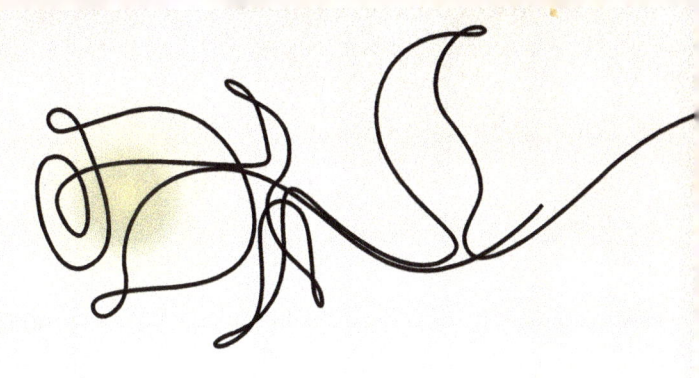

Summer

It is SO hot outside
Oh look at that, it's summer
No school for two months
Oh look, it's summer
Time to hang with the gang
Oh look, it's summer
Eating fresh watermelon at the cook-out
Oh look, it's Summer
MY POPSICLE IS MELTING!!!
Yup, it's definitely summer

Swimming at the pool
Playing with water guns
Oh look, it's summer
Summer's really cool
And I'm having lots of fun
Oh look, it's summer

Hanging out with all your friends
Hoping summer will never end
I don't want to go back to school again
But unfortunately, it is the end
of summer

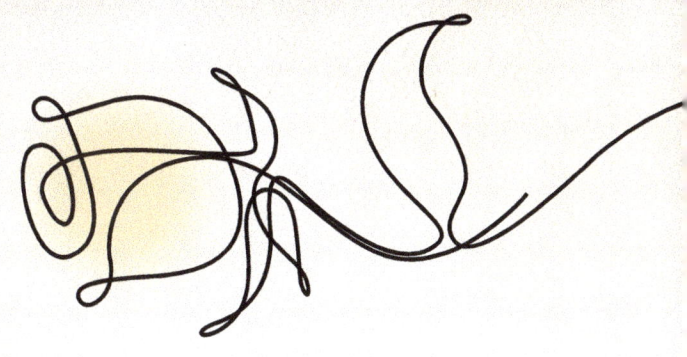

How does summer make you feel compared to other seasons?

A Beautiful Thing

Look in the mirror
What are you?
You are a beautiful thing

Who are you?
I can tell you
You are a beautiful person

What's going on inside that head of yours?

I don't know, but I know it's a beautiful thing
The mind is a beautiful thing
It creates thoughts that can take us down a path of creativity
A train full of ideas that can go in any way and take you to any
final destination

This life is a beautiful thing
Staying long enough makes you long for more

If you think hard enough, anything is a beautiful thing
You just have to see it through the right eyes

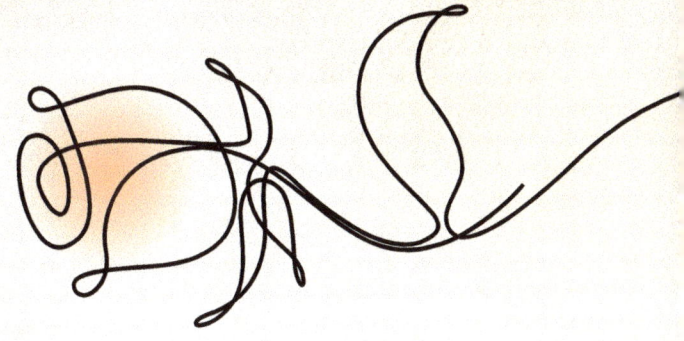

What makes you beautiful?

Just a Little Black Girl

Who's that walking down the street?
Don't mind her, she's just a little black girl
She can't do anything, she's helpless

That little black girl turns around and says
Just a little black girl? Don't belittle me
I may look little but my brain is big and so is my heart
I have feelings and I care
And right now, those feelings flash bright red saying MAD MAD MAD
Might wanna stay clear

Except she doesn't say all that
She smiles and waves and keeps walking
She is not helpless - she just has respect for those older
Even when they are wrong, address them with respect
Mom taught me that

Respect has no bounds
So I try to keep my cool
But just like school
I'm being tested
I'm a nice person
And at times I get mad

I might be just a little black girl
But I pack a big amount of confidence
And big fists which are almost never my first choice
But they chill in the back of my head
Instead I use words
I don't get physical, but I could if I wanted
It's just respect
Why get physical when you could talk it out and no one gets hurt?

She's beautiful, kind, smart, and gifted in her own ways
She is special and sometimes needs a little push
But that's ok
She's not some helpless little girl
In fact, she's smarter than those who call her that
Because she doesn't fight, she just calms down knowing that ain't
the truth
So next time you call her just a little black girl
Remember she is way more than that

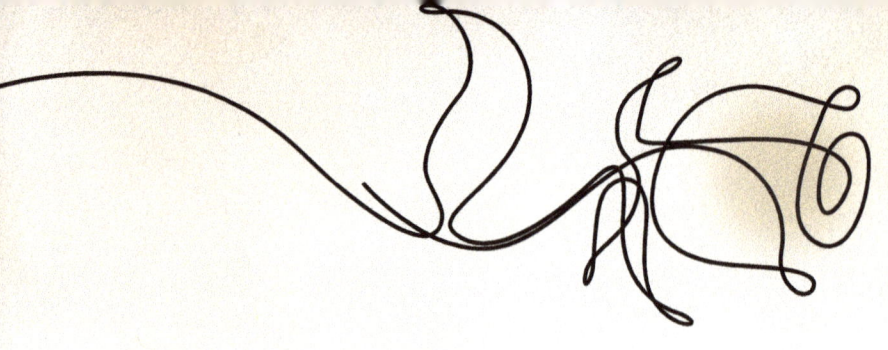

What do you wish people knew about you that they might not see on the outside?

_____
_____
_____
_____
_____
_____
_____
_____
_____
_____
_____
_____
_____
_____
_____
_____

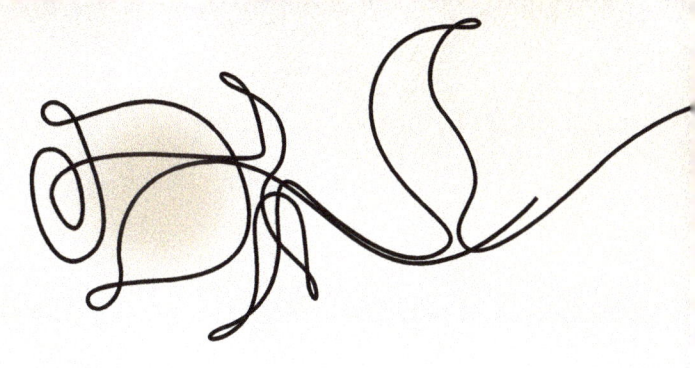

Here Today, Gone Tomorrow

Every day I wake up knowing I survived
Knowing I'm alive
But that tiny voice in my head is saying
This could be the day you die

I spend time with family and friends
And even though I'm here today, I could be gone tomorrow
I seem so present right now, but I'm in my head
Going down an endless train of thoughts
Start off random, then lead me to how could I possibly meet
my demise on an average day like this?

9/11 was an average day like this
Life-threatening pandemics started on average days like this
Deadly wars have started on average days like this
Over 160,000 people died on an average day like this

Every day I wake up knowing this could be my final day
Knowing that day will come eventually, who's stopping it
from being today or tomorrow?
I could be here today, gone tomorrow
I don't want to just disappear like that
As another person who roamed the earth for years
If my physical body is gone, I still want my presence to be there

I don't want to fade away
Fade into black and be forgotten
I want to shine and be remembered
I'm not ready to die yet
I have so much to do
So much to accomplish
So much to live for

Every day I wake up knowing I could be here today, gone tomorrow
Here Today, Gone Tomorrow
Here Today, Gone Tomorrow
Here Today, and just like that, Gone Tomorrow
I don't want to be gone tomorrow

What do you love most about your life right now?

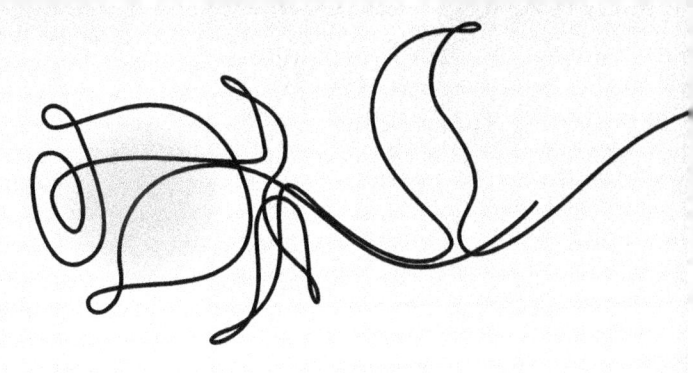

The End

Good Job!
You made it!
Made it to the end
But my poems so good, you'll want to read them again
I hope these poems were to your satisfaction
And if they weren't, oh well, I like them

They say all good things must come to end
And if you didn't know, this book is one of those good things
Life is another good thing that comes to an end
No one can escape that
But the sad things can end too

Some people may struggle with those bad things
Those emotions they keep locked up
That anger or sadness inside, about to explode
It can end

In this huge world there's a way to stop everything
I mean, who's taking the time to find the 127,000,008th digit of pi?
It has to end at some point
Eventually, the word will end
And the sun
And our galaxy and universe in total will gather and end
Everything does
Including this poem
The End!

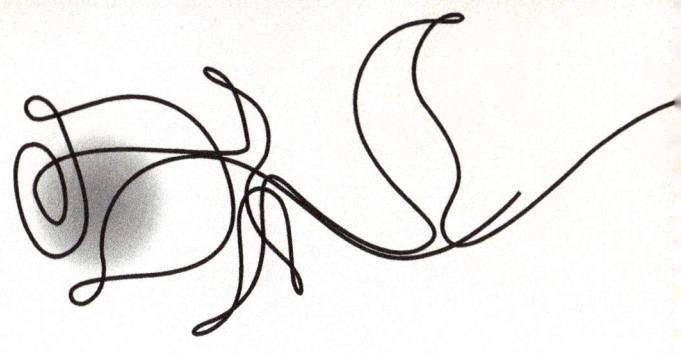

How has this poetry book helped you understand your own feelings?

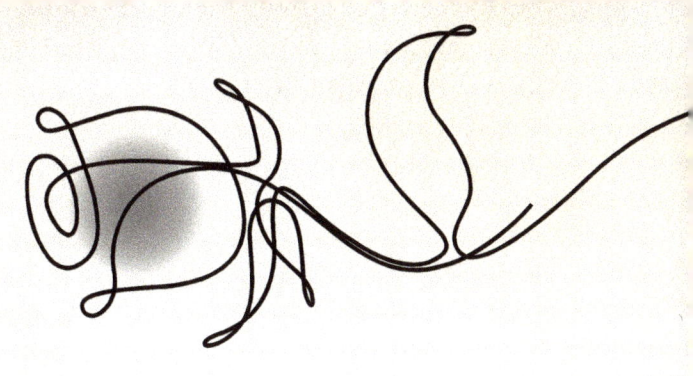

About the Author

Peace Mbuashu-Ndip

Peace is a young creative talent with roots in Cameroon, though she currently resides in the United States. The youngest of four siblings, she developed a passion for music early on, which sparked her interest in theater, dance, and playing the ukulele. Her journey as a writer began in kindergarten with her first short story. By the age of nine, Peace was writing songs, and at ten, she discovered her love for poetry. She made her stage debut in her first school play at age eleven and has since performed in additional school and church productions, as well as dance recitals. Alongside her artistic pursuits, Peace is an active member of her church youth choir, the middle school step team, and has been a dedicated Girl Scout since the age of five.